THOUGHT CATALOG BOOKS

If You Were Still Alive

If You Were Still Alive

HOLLY RIORDAN

THOUGHT CATALOG BOOKS

Brooklyn, NY

For Catherine Booth, Mike Gengo, and Mary Lanka—
I can't dance like you did, but I can write, so this is for you.

Contents

1

My World Would Be So Different If You Were Still Alive

It doesn't matter that it's been years since you've passed away. It doesn't matter that half of the people that are now in my life have never even met you. I still think about you all the time. I still wish you were here. After all, everything would be so different if you were still alive.

Of course, when I say "everything," I don't actually mean everything. Chances are, I'd still be living under the same roof and working the same job. I'd still be dating the same boy and taking care of the same dog. Only little things would change, but the little things mean the most.

If you were still alive, I wouldn't have to push the happy memories away because they're too painful to replay in my head. I'd just think of them and smile and then pick up the phone to give you a call.

If you were still alive, I'd have one more person to introduce my boyfriend to. One more person to embarrass me with awkward stories about my childhood. One more person to welcome him into our fucked up family.

If you were still alive, then there would be one more voice cheering over the fireworks on Fourth of July. One more voice yelling at the baseball game and one more voice singing along to whatever bullshit song popped on the radio.

If you were still alive, there would be one less tattoo adorning my body. One less date that made me burst into tears every single year. Your birthday would be the only date that reminded me of you, and we'd have a hell of a good time celebrating.

If you were still alive, there'd be one more person for me to call whenever I needed a designated driver. One more person to scream at me for acting like an irresponsible kid. One more person to make me feel like I'd be missed if anything ever happened to me.

If you were still alive, there would be one more invitation to send out for my wedding. One more person to dance with when the "Electric Slide" flooded through the speakers. One more person to tear up and tell me how happy they are for me and my new hubby.

If you were still alive, I'd have one more person to show around my new apartment. One more person to dog-sit for me during week-long vacations. One more person to tell me that they're proud of everything I've become.

If you were still alive, I wouldn't have to talk to you through prayers or through my dreams. I could send you a text or write you a letter or just show up on your front step in the middle of the goddamn night, and you'd be happy to listen.

If you were still alive, I wouldn't have pushed certain people away. I wouldn't be as pessimistic and cold as I am now. I wouldn't be so terrified of losing someone again, someone I care about as much as you.

But if you were still alive, I might not have realized that the whole "live each day like it's your last" mindset is legit. That I need to treasure every moment while I still can and tell my family I love them as much as possible.

As much as I miss you, I'm thankful for what you taught me while you were here and what you're continuing to teach me now that you're gone.

2

The Reality Of What It's Like To Lose A Loved One

The mornings are the worst. You wake up, and for one blissful second, you forget. For one blissful second, you believe that you're going to hear them fumbling around in the kitchen or that you're going to reach for your phone to see a text from them. For that one second, your life feels…normal.

And then you remember.

You remember that they're never going to sit down for breakfast with you or send you a drunken text. You remember that they're not going to burst through the front door or blow up your phone. You remember that all of those little moments that you took for granted are gone forever. That they're nothing but memories now.

The mornings are when you're blasted with all of the pain you felt the moment you heard they were sick, the moment the news was first delivered. Your head hearts. Your stomach hurts. Your heart hearts. It's a pain more intense than a black eye or a broken bone. You realize it's only emotional, the nerves hidden inside of you, but it doesn't matter. It still feels like you're being torn apart.

And then you have to go on with your day. The people close to you will treat you tenderly for a while, but strangers on the street won't give a damn about your problems. They won't even *know* about your problems. If you get distracted on the highway and cut someone off, you won't get a free pass. You won't be told that it's okay because you're going through a lot. To them, you'll just be the asshole who doesn't know how to drive. They have no idea what you're going through. Really, does anyone?

After a few months, after you've used up your allotted time to grieve, you have to smile, even around the people who know what you've endured. After a few months, you no longer have permission to lash out. You no longer have permission to sulk. You love someone who's dead, but *everyone* loves someone who's dead, so you're expected to get over it. You're expected to move on.

But the truth is, you'll never move on. Not really. There will be some days when you can think of them with a smile and other days when they won't even cross your mind. And some days will even feel normal again. But then there will be a day when a certain song comes on the radio, or you smell a stranger with a familiar perfume, and you'll lose control. Your tears will turn into wails and the pain will be just as vivid as it was when it was fresh.

Some days will be harder than others. But you'll survive them all.

You don't really have a choice.

3

Don't Blame Yourself For Their Death

Maybe you've already heard this a million times. Or maybe you haven't heard it at all. Either way, you need to know that it's not your fault they're gone. It's time to quiet that part of your mind that's been nagging at you, telling you that there was something you could've done in order to avoid such a tragedy. Because there isn't. Blaming yourself is irrational and it isn't going to make dealing with their death any easier.

So don't blame yourself for taking a little too long to call an ambulance. Don't blame yourself for bringing them to the wrong doctor or the wrong hospital. Don't blame yourself for not giving them the mental help they needed. Don't blame yourself for contributing to their death, because you didn't. You need to understand that. There's nothing you could've done to stop it. Nothing at all.

And while you're at it, don't blame yourself for forgetting to tell them you love them on their last day. Don't blame yourself for spending less time with them than you should've. Don't blame yourself for making them miserable for a second or a day or a week, because you brought them happiness overall. So stop dwelling on the scattering of things you did wrong.

There's no reason to bring every painful memory you can think of to the surface. They don't blame you for the way that you screamed at them when they screwed up. They don't blame you for the way you shut them out when you were sick of their whining. They don't blame you for acting distant when you had no clue what would end up happening to them. And if they don't blame you, then you shouldn't blame yourself.

You need to stop coming up with new scenarios in the middle of the night. Give the "what if"s a break. You can't go back and change what happened, so there's no sense in thinking about all of the ways you could've saved them or at least prolonged their life for a little bit longer. Mourning can mess with your mind, but don't let it convince you that you've made a fatal mistake. You're human. Not a monster. And not a superhero. You know what that means? That you couldn't have done anything. I know you wish you could've, but you couldn't have.

So instead of fantasizing about what you wish would've happened, think about what actually happened. Replay memories in your mind. The happy ones. The ones that will remind you that, even though they're gone, they made a huge impact on you while they were alive. They changed your world, and believe it or not, *you* changed *their* world.

4

I'm Terrified Of Forgetting You

Sometimes remembering you is painful, but the possibility of forgetting is even worse. I know I'll never forget your name or your birthday or what you meant to me, but I don't want to lose the little things.

I don't want to forget the exact shade of your eyes or the color of your hair. When I close my eyes, I want to be able to picture you. I want to be able to visualize every freckle and every mole. I don't want to have to flip through pictures on my phone or look at a frame on the wall to remember the way that your lips curled when you smiled. And I don't want to be forced to consult my video camera in order to remember the way that your voice sounded. I want to remember those things on my own.

I don't want to forget any of the holidays or the get-togethers from back when I was little, either. I know it's only natural for those memories to fade now that I'm older, but I'm not ready to let them go. I don't want to clasp a necklace around my neck and forget that you were the one who gave it to me. I don't want to look at old photographs and forget that you were the one holding the camera that I aimed my smile toward. I don't want to forget any of the fun memories because we can't form any new ones.

I don't want to forget any of the important pieces of your life. I don't want to forget the kind of car that you drove me around in as a kid. I don't want to forget the name of the CD that you used to keep in the glove compartment. I don't want to forget the brand of mac and cheese you used to buy. I don't want to forget the color of your bedroom walls. I don't want to forget the nicknames that you called me. I don't want to forget any of it.

But more than anything, I don't want to forget the lessons that you taught me. I don't want to forget about all of the morals you've instilled in me just because you're not around to lecture me when I screw up. I want to live life the same way I would've lived if if you were still alive—in fact, I want to live life even *better* than before, because now I have a purpose. Now I have to make you proud.

5

50 One-Sentence Reminders For When You're Struggling Without Them

1. They would rather have you remember them and smile than cry.

2. You don't have to talk about it if you don't want to.

3. The end of their life isn't the end of yours.

4. It's okay to be upset and it's okay to be afraid.

5. They knew you loved them, even if you never said it.

6. You're strong enough to survive this.

7. You made it through yesterday and you can make it through today.

8. You're not alone, even if it feels like you are.

9. You were one of the reasons why they loved life.

10. You're allowed to be angry.

11. The only reason it hurts is because you had someone truly special in your life.

12. Emotional pain is just as valid as physical pain.

13. Be thankful that you have plenty of pictures to remember them by.

14. Your tears aren't a sign of weakness.

15. Live your best life as a "thank you" to them.

16. They're dead, but they're not gone because they're still in your heart.

17. Never be afraid to love again.

18. Let music help you heal.

19. Every single day will be a tiny bit easier than the last.

20. You look beautiful, even when you cry.

21. Everyone mourns in different ways.

22. One day, you'll be able to talk about them without bursting into tears.

23. Your relationship with them isn't over just because their life is over.

24. It's okay to stay in bed all day.

25. No one else understands exactly how you're feeling, but they *are* there for you.

26. Everyone has lost someone.

27. You're allowed to be confused.

28. You couldn't have done anything to save them.

29. Pain makes you stronger.

30. They loved you until their last breath.

31. Life should be measured in laughs, not in years.

32. If you're at your lowest now, there's nowhere to go but up.

33. They're proud of you.

34. Not even death can erase them from your memories.

35. Be thankful they were in your life, even if it was only for a little while.

36. Love never dies.

37. They will always hold a special place in your heart.

38. There's beauty hidden in pain.

39. You're still alive, so make the most of it.

40. You can still talk to them at their grave or whilst looking up at the sky.

41. You'll learn to live without them.

42. Don't feel guilty when you're ready to move on.

43. You're not alone in your mourning, so there are plenty of shoulders to cry on.

44. Even baby steps are better than standing still.

45. Death is a mystery to us, so as far as we know, it might be better than life.

46. If you can get through this, you can get through anything.

47. Don't let *their* death ruin *your* life.

48. They want you to stop crying.

49. They want you to be happy.

50. Use them as a reminder to spend time with your other loved ones while you still can.

6

I Wish My Boyfriend Would've Met You

I wish you didn't die so soon. That way, you would've had the chance to meet the person I'm planning on spending the rest of my life with. You would've been able to hug him and ask him about his job and warn him not to hurt me.

He knows your name. He knows what you look like. He knows all about you. But no matter how many times I mention you, he'll never really *know* you. It's impossible for him to understand what type of person you were when he never got the chance to have a conversation with you.

I can show him pictures, but what do looks matter? A photograph can show him your smile, but it won't show him the second before or after the smile. It won't show him what you were smiling at. It won't accurately portray you.

That's why I tell him so many stories. It's the best way for him to get a handle on your personality, on who you truly were. But even the stories aren't going to do the job. I can't tell them the right way. I can explain what you said and how you said it, but I can't explain the important things. The way your face looked. The way your voice sounded. I can picture the scenes in my mind, but I can't turn the images into words.

Even video recordings won't help because they're still a second hand experience. I don't want him to watch you talking to someone else. I want *him* to talk to you. I don't want him to hear you sing to the baby version of me on my birthday. I want him to hear you sing to him on *his* birthday.

I know you would've gotten along with him. I know you would've made him laugh when you swapped stories about the idiotic things I've done in the past. I know that you would've loved him as much as I love him.

I know it's impossible for you two to cross paths. I know asking for it sounds whiny. Greedy, even. But I wish the person I loved the most as a child would be able to meet the person I love the most as an adult. I wish that I'd get to put out an extra chair at my wedding and leave time for an extra speech.

To him, you're fiction. A story. A name. I hate that he only sees you as a ghost instead of as a flesh-and-blood human, because to me you're still around. You'll always be there. And I hate that I can't share you with him.

7

I'm (Not) Sorry I Never Visit Your Grave

It's not that I don't love you. It's not that I don't miss you. I think it's clear I do. But I don't want to sit on a dead plot of grass in front of a hunk of rock with words scribbled across it. Those vague words don't actually describe you. *Loving mother. Caring father. Beloved brother.* What does any of that actually mean? They're the same words that are written on every other tombstone in the area. What distinguishes your tombstone from someone else's? Nothing.

No one knows who you *really* are just by looking at your grave. I know who you are because you're hidden in my heart. So I'm sorry, but I don't want to pluck the weeds off of your grave and then sit over your decomposing body. I care more about your spirit, and your spirit goes wherever I go. I can talk to you from my bedroom or from inside of my car. I don't have to wait until I'm in the graveyard to have a conversation.

Staring at your tombstone doesn't remind me of you. It reminds me of your funeral. It reminds me of the day when we lowered your body into the ground. Of the day when I was crying my eyes out. Of the day when I was at my absolute lowest. Now why the hell would I want to think about that?

When I think about you, I want to think about the fun times we had. I want to think about you when you're happy and healthy. I don't want to picture the pale, rigid skin of your corpse. I want to picture the way your face lit up whenever you laughed. I don't want to picture the perfectly painted nails folded over your chest. I want to think of the chipped nails that used to high five me and help me comb through my hair. I want to think of the real you. Not your body. Not your death. *You.*

That's why I'm not going to apologize for driving past the graveyard without stopping to stare. I'm not going to apologize for letting the grass grow instead of placing flowers there on holidays. And on your birthday, I'm going to look at your old pictures and sing to you from my kitchen. I'll celebrate your life, but I'll do it on my own terms.

I understand why other people visit the graves of their loved ones, and I respect it. I find it sweet. Charming. But I personally don't have any reason to visit your grave. It wouldn't make me feel any better. It would only make me feel worse, and it's already hard enough to deal with your death as it is.

So if you don't mind, I'm going to continue to talk to you from afar instead of traveling to the place that reminds me of the worst day of my life. I'm going to continue to remember you as a living person instead of as a dead body.

8

This Is When I Think About You

I think of you whenever there's a funeral scene on TV. When an actor is sprawled out in a hospital bed, taking his last breaths. When a casket is being lowered into the ground. When families are dressed in black and shedding counterfeit tears. I don't see an actor playing some fictional character that doesn't mean a thing to me. I see you. I always see you.

I think of you during the big moments of my life, every time I hit a new milestone. When I graduate, when I get promoted, when I eventually get married. I think of you and wonder what type of card you would've gotten me or what type of cake you would've baked me to celebrate. I wonder where you would've taken me out for dinner and drinks. But I don't have to wonder if you're proud of me, because I already know that you are.

I think of you whenever *your* music comes on the radio, the type that used to make you jump up and drag everyone up along with you so you didn't have to dance alone. It doesn't matter if the music that pops on is upbeat or if it tells a story that has absolutely nothing to do with my memories of you, because I don't hear a word of the lyrics. At least, I don't hear the singer. I just hear *your* voice singing along. I hear your feet sliding across the floor. I hear you grumbling when everyone else complains about how sucky your taste is.

I think of you whenever I smell the scent of the candles you used to keep around the house. Whenever I get a taste of your favorite beer. Whenever a rerun of your favorite show comes on. Whenever your favorite breed of dog scampers down the street. Your favorite things are now my favorite things, even if I legitimately don't like them. I just *feel* like I do because they bring me closer to you.

I think of you whenever I step into the room that you used to call your own. It looks different now. There's a little too much dust in the spot where you would've been picking up and putting down your cell phone each night and there's a little too much color on the walls. But most of all, it's a little too empty.

I think of you whenever I hear about a friend losing a loved one. When I imagine what they're going through, I'm actually just thinking back to what I went through when I lost you. The pain I feel over their loss isn't due to me being *such a good friend*. It's selfishness. I'm acting like I feel sorry for that friend, which is only a version of the truth. Mostly, I'm feeling sorry for myself all over again. Their loss triggers my memories of you. It makes me miss you even more than I already do. It makes me wish you were back in my life again.

9

The Worst Part Is Watching Everyone Else Deal With Death

Your death was difficult for all of us. You had family members that didn't deserve to go through the pain of losing you, and I'm not just talking about myself. I'm talking about the people that were even closer to you (or equally as close) as I am. The people who saw you every single day. The people that loved you even more than they loved themselves.

As much as I hate crying, as much as I hate being seen crying, it's even worse to see them cry. To offer them empty words that mean something and nothing all at once.

You're in a better place.

You're looking down at them and smiling.

If there's anything I can do…

No matter what words I say or how many hugs I give, I still feel helpless. When I catch them crying, do I wrap my arms around them and squeeze? Do I tell them a funny story in an attempt to turn the tears into laughter? Or do I pretend that I didn't notice them crying and give them the privacy that they need?

How am I supposed to help them deal with something that I'm struggling with myself? I can't. But I have to try. I have to pretend to be strong. I have to act like everything is going to be okay so that the people around me will start to believe it. I have to set an example.

Because if I cry, it won't make them feel less alone. They already have plenty of people surrounding them with tears. They don't need to add me to the list. If they see me break down, then it'll only make them cry harder.

No, I have to act stoic. But I can't act heartless. I can't pretend that you meant nothing to me, that your death hasn't impacted me at all, because then everyone will know I'm playing a part, that I'm putting on an act. I need to make my attitude believable. I need to find the balance between frailty and strength.

So, instead of making everyone around me even more miserable, I'll make them laugh by recounting funny stories from your past. And instead of pointing out the pictures where you look the most beautiful, the ones that remind us of what a big loss we've endured, I'll point out the funny ones, the ones that tell a story. Funny story after funny story. Happy memory after happy memory. Gradually replacing the frowns with smiles.

It might kill me to play make-believe; it might ruin my

chances of ever getting closure, but it's something I have to do. Because the only thing worse than death is watching the people you love deal with it.

10

100 Ways To Honor Your Loved Ones After They Pass

1. Have your favorite picture of them turned into a painting.

2. Get a tattoo in their handwriting.

3. Create a stepping stone for them in your garden.

4. Name a star after them.

5. Create a scrapbook with photos of them.

6. Have their Instagram pictures printed and framed.

7. Wear their favorite necklace.

8. Make a playlist of songs that remind you of them.

9. Write a poem about them.

10. Pour out a beer for them.

11. Fill a jar with your favorite memories of them.

12. Adopt their pet.

13. Dedicate a song to them on the radio.

14. Donate to a charity in their name.

15. Volunteer for an organization they supported.

16. Keep in touch with their friends.

17. Put a bumper sticker on your car in honor of them.

18. Learn their favorite song on guitar.

19. Buy a bracelet with charms that remind you of them.

20. Save their wedding ring (or dress) for when you get married.

21. Turn their ashes into fireworks.

22. Write a song about them.

23. Fill a shadow box with things that they loved.

24. Name your pet after them.

25. Send a balloon (with a note) up to them.

26. Make your favorite picture of them your profile picture.

27. Wear a locket with their picture hidden inside.

28. Write a memoir for them.

29. Put together a video montage.

30. Dedicate a book to them.

31. Take care of the plants they left behind.

32. Name a highway after them.

33. Write a status about them on their birthday.

34. Make your favorite picture of them your phone background.

35. Leave a flower arrangement on their grave.

36. Create a memory box filled with items that remind you of them.

37. Spread their ashes over a spot they loved.

38. Pray to them.

39. Purchase a mass card for them.

40. Light a candle for them.

41. Think about them everyday.

42. Pull the weeds at their grave.

43. Read their favorite book.

44. Place a name plaque on a bench.

45. Get a tattoo with the coordinates of their house.

46. Sponsor a brick for them.

47. Visit their favorite vacation spot.

48. Make a quilt out of their old shirts.

49. Hang up their diploma in your room.

50. Plant a tree for them.

51. Get a tattoo of their favorite quote.

52. Create a cookbook filled with their favorite recipes.

53. Have their ashes turned into a diamond.

54. Watch their favorite movie.

55. Tell funny stories about them.

56. Randomly visit their grave.

57. Wear their dog tags.

58. Share a Throwback Thursday picture with them on Instagram.

59. Use their name as a password.

60. Carry a keychain with their name on it.

61. Run in a marathon to raise money to prevent what they died of.

62. Leave a birthday card on their grave.

63. Get a tattoo of their favorite animal.

64. Have their ashes launched into space.

65. Donate their clothing to charity.

66. Put all of their pictures on a flash drive.

67. Sing their favorite song at karaoke.

68. Turn their clothing into a pillowcase.

69. Hang up a stocking with their name on it.

70. Keep their stuffed animal on your shelf.

71. Get a tattoo of their name.

72. Create a signature scent that reminds you of them.

73. Name a boat after them.

74. Leave a chair out for them for your wedding.

75. Wear their favorite baseball cap.

76. Mention them when you're asked to give a speech.

77. Plant their favorite flowers in your garden.

78. Name your child after them.

79. Frame an item of their clothing.

80. Eat at their favorite restaurant on their birthday.

81. Release floating lanterns for them.

82. Keep their prayer card in your pocket.

83. Engage in an activity that they loved.

84. Call up one of their closest friends to see how they've been.

85. Read through their old Tweets and Facebook posts.

86. Have their ashes placed in an hour glass.

87. Hang up an ornament with their name on it.

88. Have their ashes turned into a vinyl record.

89. Have a picnic or a piece of cake on their grave for their birthday.

90. Spend time with other people that loved them.

91. Buy a personalized mug with their picture on it.

92. Make a drawing of them.

93. Leave a knickknack that they owned on your nightstand.

94. Create a website in honor of them.

95. Sing for them on their birthday.

96. Learn to cook their favorite meal.

97. Buy a personalized phone case with their picture on it.

98. Save all of the old cards they bought you.

99. Have a moment of silence for them on holidays.

100. Live your best life so that they'll be proud of you.

11

Why Did It Have To Be You?

Why did someone as sweet as you have to be ripped away from me? There are monsters in this world, sad excuses for human beings with no heart and no one that loves them, and yet you're the one that was taken away. It just doesn't seem fair. And it's not.

Why couldn't your death have waited a few more months, a few more years, a few more decades? Why did it have to be before I found my forever person, the one I wanted to introduce you to? Before I landed my dream job, the one that would finally lead me to success? I wanted you to be proud of me. I wanted you to hear about how far I've come from over the phone instead of by eavesdropping on my prayers.

Why did it have to happen the way that it did? It could've been less painful. It could've been less sudden. If it happened in some other way, then maybe it would've been easier for me to deal with. Of course, that's probably a lie. Even if you calmly slipped away in your sleep at the age of 99, I'd still have complaints. I'd still say it wasn't fair.

Why did I assume that you'd always be there, even though I'm old enough to know the way that the universe works, even though I knew that every single life ends? I'm not stupid. I know the risks of being human. But I still didn't want to believe that the inevitable would happen to you. It was too horrible to think about back then, and it's too horrible to come to terms with now.

Why didn't I appreciate you while you were still here? Yes, I loved you. I told you and I showed you. But did I do it enough? No, of course not. I took you for granted because that's what people do. They don't understand how much their family members and friends mean to them. Not until it's too late.

Why did I have to love you so much? If I didn't give a damn about you then your death wouldn't be an issue. I would blink and be able to move on. But no, you had to be one of the most loving and caring people that I've ever met. You had to shower me with affection and drown me with your friendship. You had to make me love you.

Why aren't you here? There are so many people that wish that you were, that would give anything in order to see you again. The fact that you're gone just doesn't make any sense to me. It never did and I don't think it ever will.

12

I'm A Different Person Now That You're Dead

I wish I could say the only way I've changed is *for the better*. That the silver lining of your death is that I learned to have a newfound appreciation of life. Even though I'm trying my best to live in the moment and treat everyone I love with an insane amount of affection, it's difficult to keep up the act. I want to enjoy life, but it's far easier for me to slip into a depression where I hate the world and everything in it.

The biggest ways I've changed aren't *for the better*. Now that you're dead, I have abandonment issues. I'm terrified of getting close to someone and then having them yanked away from me. Maybe they'll leave me. Maybe they'll grow bored of me. Or maybe they'll die unexpectedly, just like you did. I don't want to go through what I went through with you again because once was bad enough. I don't know how I would survive it twice.

Now that you're dead, I worry too much. When someone I love takes a little too long to text me back or to arrive home, I assume the worst. After losing you, I've become paranoid that everyone I love will get taken away from me one by one. That death will snatch them away in the same way that it snatched you.

And now, I try a little too hard to be careful. I don't want to drive too fast and end up smashing my car into a tree. I don't want to drink too much and get alcohol poisoning. I don't want to piss off a stranger and get shot in the head. I'm so worried about death that I'm forgetting to live. I'm forgetting to do the one thing that your death was meant to teach me and *enjoy the moment.*

Of course, now that you're dead, I'm also more independent. I'm trying to learn how to take care of myself, so that I can survive on my own. I want to *want* to be alone. I want to lock myself away so that I can't get attached to anyone else. At the end of the day, I can't count on anyone else to be there for me. The only consistency is death. Either the people I love will die or I'll die, and I don't know which option is worse.

I don't know what comes after life, either—if I'll be able to watch my loved ones from the skies. But I don't want to see them suffer. I don't want to watch them break down in tears because my body was unable to support me anymore. I don't want to be the sole reason for their suffering.

I don't want to hurt them in the same way that you hurt me.

<u>13</u>

These Are The Memories That Hurt The Most

I can't stop myself from thinking about you. Even if I could, I wouldn't let the images fade and float away. I don't care how badly the memories sting. I never want to forget you. I want to hold on to the lilt of your laugh and the shade of your eyes. I refuse to let go of you and everything you meant to me.

But I hate thinking about you in your last hours. I hate thinking about the way you looked with your arms crossed over your chest, resting in your plush velvet casket. But those memories, the heart-wrenching ones where your body and soul are already disconnected, aren't the most painful memories.

The most painful memories are the ones that used to be my favorites. The ones where you're sitting side-by-side with me, having some mundane conversation about work or school. The ones where you're holding the phone to your ear, blabbering away. Where you're telling crappy jokes. Where you're drunk. Where you're laughing. Where you're dancing. Where you're cooking. Where you're singing. Where you're the most *you*. Those are the memories that remind me of why I loved you.

But those aren't the only memories that hurt. The embarrassing ones, the ones that you'd be mortified that I've been thinking about, are just as painful. The time you slipped on ice. The time you dented your car. The time you nearly set the kitchen on fire. Those are the types of memories that make me roll my eyes and call you an idiot. The ones that remind me of how real you once were. The ones that let me treat you like a person who's still here instead of an untouchable spirit in the sky I'm meant to speak highly about. You were a real person with real thoughts and real flaws. You were human. You were just like me.

And then there are the 'last' memories. The last time I celebrated a birthday with you. The last thing I said to you. The last time I hugged you. The last time I told you I loved you. The worst part is that I don't remember most of those moments. I hate myself for it, but it proves how big of my life you were. You were always around. You were always *there*, so why would I pay attention to little things like that? I didn't think they mattered back then.

I thought you'd always be around.

14

I Miss You Even More Now That I'm Older

When I was younger, I don't think I realized it. Even though everyone told me what had happened, drilled the idea of death into my head, it still didn't feel real. It felt more like you were on vacation. Or like you snuck away to join the witness protection program. Like you were far away from us but still flitting around somewhere. Part of me thought that you would return one day with a smile on your face, laughing about how ridiculous it was that we believed you were permanently gone.

And when I was younger, I unquestionably believed that my loved ones were in heaven, waiting to see me again. Now it doesn't really matter whether I believe in heaven or not, because no matter where I stand on the subject, I know that there's a *possibility* that I'm wrong. I know that there's no guarantee. The afterlife isn't as black and white as I always thought it was.

That's why, now that I'm older, the permanency of your death is just starting to hit me. And it feels like I'm losing you all over again.

Now that I'm older, I realize how *young* you were. You weren't supposed to come face to face with death. We live in an age with unlimited medication and educated doctors and a high life expectancy. So why did the unexpected have to happen to you?

Now that I'm older, I realize why people have drilled "live every day like it's your last" into my head. Songs say it, movies teach it, and celebrities preach it, because it's the truth. There's no guarantee that I'm going to wake up the next morning, so I might as well enjoy my time on earth while I can. I can't stop myself from dying, but I can encourage myself to live.

Now that I'm older, I realize what a tragedy it is that you've missed out on so many different birthdays and weddings and babies. There are so many milestones that people would've loved to have you around for. There are so many unbought gifts and unheard congratulations.

Now that I'm older, I realize why so many people are terrified of dying. They think that it's going to be just as painful for them as it is for their loved ones that have to deal with the aftermath. They think that the pain they endure will be just as intense as the pain they inflict.

And, now that I'm older, I realize how much you meant to me. People like you don't come along often. In fact, no one like you has come along since your death. I don't think they ever will. You're one of a kind. And I miss you like hell.

15

Holidays Suck Without You

When December rolls around, I don't even know what the point is in celebrating. You were just one piece of the family, a single soul. And yet after you died, everything changed. The dynamic shifted into something bittersweet. We all know where you are, so we can't pretend that you're just stuck at work or hidden inside the bathroom. Whenever the family gets together now, your absence is heavy. After all, it's not really *the family* without you.

Everything that I once loved about our get-togethers have become something to loathe. I used to drink to form fun new memories, but now I drink to forget. The conversations used to be about how successful our futures would be and now the conversations are about how wonderful our past was.

I honestly don't know how to handle the holiday season. I'm stuck between carrying on traditions and letting them die with you. I don't want to insult you by giving up the customs that you pushed me to follow ever since I was a kid. But it doesn't feel right to continue them without you, either. To me, tradition isn't really about *what* we're doing. It's about whom I'm doing it with. So now that you're gone, what's the point?

It doesn't feel right to take pictures at family gatherings, either. To have everyone wrap their arms around each other and snap photos that supposedly contain *everyone*. It's a sweet sentiment, one that I understand, but we're never going to be able to take a proper family photo again. We don't have enough bodies. We don't have you.

And then I have to deal with the movies, those family-friendly films about how our relatives are the important thing in the world, that run from October all the way until December. I understand why people enjoy them, but I don't need a reminder of how much I'm missing out on. I don't need those movies, which are made to put a smile on our face, to turn me into a moping mess. Some people might call me a Grinch, but those are the people who still have their families intact.

The worst part is that I'm still not used to the emptiness of my shopping cart. As stingy as I am, I hate buying fewer presents. When you were alive, I could search for hours and still be stuck on what to get. But now that you're gone, shopping seems so easy. Everywhere I look, there's a movie or a book that I know you would love.

Everywhere I look, I see you.

<u>16</u>

Losing A Pet Is Just As Bad As Losing A Person

They were the first one to greet you, tail wagging, when you came home. They were the first one to notice when you were upset, even if you tried not to show it on your face. And they were the *only* one that would keep the secrets you whispered into their floppy ears.

They ate dinner with you and slept in your bed with you. They kept you company when your friends went out without you. They fought with you. They played with you. They cuddled with you. They made you feel like you were *needed*.

Humans are disgusting creatures. But dogs? They don't have any flaws. Sure, they might be missing a patch or fur or have a habit of ripping up the carpet, but they're never going to hurt you. They're never going to betray you or disappoint you like a human could. Pets are the purest creatures on the planet.

Watching your dog die is the worst kind of pain imaginable. They can't tell you how much they love you. They can't reassure you that you're going to be okay without them. They can't remind you of all of the fun times you had. They can only look up at you, lick your face, and make it abundantly clear that they love you.

Because they *do* love you, in a different way than a human ever could. Humans always have ulterior motives. They love you in the hopes of getting laid or getting rich or being loved back. But dogs? They only want to make you happy. When you're excited, they're excited. When you're sad, they're sad. They're not just pets. They're not just family members. They're a part of you.

You never realize how strong silence can be until after you lose a dog. No nails scraping against the wooden floors. No barking when another animal pops up on the television. No begging to go outside at two in the morning or yipping in excitement when you walk through the door. Without them, your house will feel empty. Unlivable.

The biggest lie in the world is that pets are replaceable. Getting another dog won't plug the hole in your heart. Sure, you'll be happy to have a new furry friend scampering around, but you'll still miss the one that's vanished.

You won't ever get over losing a pet. Your childhood dog will mean as much to you as the dog you get when you're married and the dog sitting next to you right now. Because dogs are irreplaceable. Their deaths are just as heartbreaking as any human's. Sometimes, they're even worse.

<u>17</u>

The Truth About The Five Stages Of Grief

1. Denial

This happens the moment you first hear the news. Maybe you received a phone call. Maybe you saw the look in another family member's eye, and knew what they had to tell you before they had the chance to say it. Or maybe you were there, right there, when it happened.

But even if you saw it with your own eyes, you still don't believe it. You swear it's impossible. You just saw them. You just talked to them. They were just alive.

The tears don't come yet. They come later, once the truth sinks in. Right now, you're in denial. You think that there must've been a mistake. That their eyes are going to flick open at any moment. That there's no way you've actually lost them.

2. Anger

You yell at the doctors, because they're incompetent assholes that must not have been doing their job correctly. You yell at the janitor that bumps you in the hospital hall, because they're obviously a bastard with no consideration for other people.

You even yell at the person you lost, because they were in the wrong place at the wrong time. Or because they shouldn't have injected that needle. Or because they shouldn't have taken that highway. Or waited so long to get a check-up. But mostly, you yell, because they shouldn't have let go yet. They shouldn't have left you.

3. Bargaining

If you bring them back, I swear I'll never drink again. I'll never smoke again. I'll pray to you every night. I'll go to church every Sunday. Just bring them back. Take me instead. Bring them back and take me with you.

Even if you're an atheist, even if the idea of God sounds asinine to you, you still find yourself talking to Him. Begging him for a redo. You'll do anything to get them back, even if it includes babbling to the sky. You just want to make things right. You try to do everything that you can, and right now, bargaining is the only thing you can think of.

4. Depression

It's finally there. The red eyes. The stuffed nose. The sobs. The sadness might set in during the wake when you're wrapped in the arms of other people that loved them. When you finally see them in the casket, still and silent. When you see the photos plastered around the room, from back when they were healthy.

Or it might set in at night when you're alone in your room, during those first moments you have to yourself. You've been so busy with funeral plans and never-ending phone calls that you haven't had any time to think, but alone in your room, you have hours to climb inside your head. To remember. And remembering hurts.

Or your grief might set in months later when you see a car on the road, the same type that they used to drive you around with when you were a kid. When you realize that you can't call them and tell them about the coincidence, because they aren't around to hear, you'll break down. No one knows when the depression is going to kick in, but it always comes, and it destroys you.

5. Acceptance

Eventually, you'll accept what happened, but acceptance doesn't mean what you think it means. It doesn't mean you're back to living life the same way you were before it all went downhill. It just means you've gotten used to talking about them in the past tense instead of the present. You're still not okay with the fact that they're gone. You're just used to it.

18

No One Realizes You're Doing These Things Out Of Grief

1. Wearing *that* necklace. Or bracelet. Or ring.

You might get teased about it. Your friends might ask you why the hell you wear the same piece of jewelry day after day. They might tell you how ugly it is or how it's about time for you to buy something new. But you're never going to take it off. It doesn't matter if it matches your outfit. It doesn't matter if it gets rusted. It doesn't matter if the color fades. It doesn't matter if it looks like complete and utter shit.

Why? Because it used to belong to them. And even though they're in your heart, and they'll always be in your heart, you need something physical. Since their body isn't there, their jewelry is the next best thing. It's what makes you feel safe. Loved. At home.

2. Staying away from certain music.

You used to love Country music, but now you can't listen to it without the tears flowing, because that was their favorite genre. It was the type that they used to play during every holiday party, and you can't think back to the holidays without thinking of them.

And you can't listen to any of the songs that they played during the wake or the funeral or the get together you had afterward. You can't listen to the theme song from their favorite show. You can't even listen to certain songs on the radio, songs that they never got the chance to hear because you know they would've loved them.

3. Hating on holidays.

For the first time in your life, you're not excited for December to roll around. You won't tell anyone the reason why, so all of your quasi-friends and coworkers will call you a Grinch. They'll accuse you of being a drag for the fun of it, because they don't realize there's a deeper meaning behind your bitterness.

And then there will be other people, the ones who understand but suffocate you with their kindness. They'll invite you over for a turkey dinner with their family, but their family isn't a replacement for yours. You'd rather be alone than spend the holiday pretending. Pretending to smile. Pretending to be happy. Pretending that everything is okay.

4. Avoiding social media.

You don't want to see all the sorry-for-your-loss messages on your Facebook page. You don't want to see the posts from family members that didn't give a crap about the person you lost while they were alive, the ones that are suddenly composing statuses about what a great person they are not that they're dead.

And there's no way in hell you're going to check Instagram on holidays. The only picture you could post is a throwback, and that's just depressing. You don't want to upload old pictures of your mom smiling for the camera on Mother's Day when everyone else is posting current pictures with their moms. The mom that's sitting right next to them. It just doesn't seem fair. You don't want any part of it.

5. Randomly lashing out.

It doesn't matter how long it's been since their death. Every once in a while, the memories will flare up, and instead of getting upset, you'll get pissed off. Irrationally bitter. So you'll snap. You'll cut off another car and then stick your middle finger up when they honk at you. You'll yell at your partner for forgetting to do the dishes, even though it's actually your turn. You'll yell at your roommate just for breathing too loud.

And if you told them the truth, if you admitted why you were in such a bad mood, they'd let things slide. But you refuse to admit it. You don't want to say. For some reason, it's embarrassing to admit the truth. But why? Because you should be over it by now? Because you think grief makes you weak? You don't know the answer.

6. Clamming up during certain conversations.

If you just lost your father and then your best friend brags about how her dad just bought her a new car, it'll be hard to stop yourself from getting upset. If you just lost your sister and hear someone complaining about how their sibling won't stop texting them, then you'll be just as upset. It's hard to deal with the fact that your family has fallen apart when you have friends with two parents and a household of siblings that don't even appreciate it.

But it's just as bad when they purposely leave things out. When they realize that they just mentioned their grand-mother right after you lost your grandmother and immedi-ately switched the subject. You're thankful that they're trying to spare your feelings, but it also pisses you off. You don't want their pity. You just want to feel okay again.

19

I Want To Drink A Beer With You

Forget weddings. Forget birthdays. Forget promotions. Forget all of those major milestones. It sucks that you won't be there during the big moments in my life, but I'm more concerned about the little things. I want you to be with me on lazy afternoons and on random weekends, during the mundane moments.

I want you to lounge around in my living room after cracking open the beer that I handed you. I want you to comment on how I'm so cheap and never spring for the expensive stuff. I want you to tease me about how many candles I own and the fact that I still haven't picked out curtains to cover the windows. I want you to joke around with me, because we're comfortable enough to do that.

I want you to tell me boring stories during which I'll drift off. I want to hear about the fish you caught with your brand new lure that I'll never remember the name of. I want to hear about the new flowers you planted in your garden that are already blooming. I want you to tell me about how your neighbors are so fucking nosy and about how you can't believe how much the Mets suck this year. I just want to hear you talk. About everything. About nothing.

And I want you to ask me about my life, even though I don't have anything interesting to say. I want to tell you about the new person I'm dating and the concert we went to a few days earlier. I want to tell you about how much I love my new job and what project I've been working on. I want to talk to you about the most boring parts of my life. I just want a normal day with you.

I want you to be here, in my house, filling it with your scent. I want to hear you fumbling around in the kitchen, trying to find where I stored the rest of the drinks. I want to hear your voice and your laugh and the sound of your footsteps.

I want you to tell me it's fine when my dog jumps up on you and starts licking your hand. I want you to pet him and search for a ball to toss him. I want you to make fun of me again, this time for how chubby he is and how I should really stop being lazy and start taking him on more walks. I want you to tell me that you're planning on stealing him when you're on your way out the door.

And when you leave, I want you to wrap your arms around me and squeeze. I don't want to settle for one of those quick hugs I used to give when you were alive. I want a real one. A long one. One that will hold me over until I see you again.

20

Get A Tattoo In Honor Of Your Loved One

You can't listen to their favorite song on a constant loop. You can't drive their old car for the rest of your adult life. And even though you wear their necklace everyday, it's going to break eventually. If you want a permanent token to remember them by, then you need to get a tattoo in honor of them.

You don't have to get a cross down your leg. You don't have to get an angel printed on your ankle or rosary beads across your back. If you want to go big, you can, but your tattoo doesn't have to be anything crazy. You can get a hummingbird on your arm, because it was their favorite animal. You can get a four-leaf clover behind your ear because they were Irish. You can get something small, something non-religious, that's significant.

Think about their favorite things. Their favorite flower. Their favorite hobby. Their favorite vacation spot. Try to come up with a tattoo design that will make you smile whenever you look at it. Something that describes their personality perfectly.

That way, whenever you're missing them, you don't have to find a photo of them in your phone or search your room for their prayer card. You can just look down at your tattoo and feel their presence. You can run your hands over your skin and imagine that they haven't left your side. Even the smallest tattoo can give you back some of the strength that their death took away.

It can make you feel like they still have more in store for you. They aren't around to warn you to stay away from that asshole you have a crush on or to encourage you to go after your dream job, but whenever you need guidance, you can look at your tattoo and think about what they would say. You can get advice from them beyond the grave.

A tattoo won't scar your body. It will enhance it. It will add a beautiful memory to an otherwise empty canvas of skin. And there's no need to wonder how you'll feel about it ten years down the line, because a memorial tattoo isn't something you're ever going to regret. Why? Because you're never going to lose the love you have for that person. You're never going to want to wash them away from your mind or from your skin.

Don't worry about the sensation you'll feel as the needle drags across your skin. It will be painless compared to the emotional turmoil you suffered through after they died. Besides, the end result will be worth it. You can handle it. You've handled worse things.

So if you want to keep their memory alive, get them tattooed onto your skin in the same way they're tattooed onto your heart.

21

30 Modern Songs To Listen To When You Want A Good Cry

Some days, it's best to avoid anything that reminds you of the person you've lost. But on other days, all you'll want to do is grab a box of tissues and let the tears out. When that somber mood strikes, it's a good idea to have a few sad songs on your playlist.

1. "Drink a Beer" by Luke Bryan

2. "Brother" by Falling in Reverse

3. "Gone Too Soon" by Simple Plan

4. "I Drive your Truck" by Lee Brice

5. "When I'm Gone" by Eminem

6. "Bye Bye" by Mariah Carey

7. "Believe" by The All-American Rejects

8. "Tonight" by FM Static

9. "Over You" by Miranda Lambert

10. "Hear You Me" by Jimmy Eat World

11. "Slipped Away" by Avril Lavigne

12. "Cancer" by My Chemical Romance

13. Here Comes Goodbye by Rascal Flatts

14. "Song for Dad" by Keith Urban

15. "View from Heaven" by Yellowcard

16. "The Greatest Man I Never Knew" by Reba McEntire

17. "I Miss You" by Miley Cyrus

18. "See You Again" by Carrie Underwood

19. "What Sarah Said" by Death Cab For Cutie

20. "Whiskey Lullaby" by Brad Paisley

21. "Hurt" by Christina Aguilera

22. "I'll Be Missing You" by Puff Daddy

23. "My Baby Blue" by Dave Matthews Band

24. "Terrible Things" by Mayday Parade

25. "Don't Take the Girl" by Tim McGraw

26. "J.A.R." by Green Day

27. "Who Knew?" by P!nk

28. "Live in the Sky" by T.I.

29. "Fly" by Celine Dion

30. "To Where You Are" by Josh Groban

22

What No One Tells You About Dealing With Death

They don't tell you how strange it feels to get ready for a wake or a funeral. Do you have to run out to buy black dress shoes? Is the outfit you picked out appropriate? How should you do your hair? You feel guilty if you try to look good, because you're not going to a party. You're not going to a club. But you're still expected to look nice. Even if you're falling apart internally, you're meant to *look* put together. Your outfit is the last thing you want to think about, but you have to think about it—at least a little.

They don't tell you how you feel like you're on display during the wake and the funeral. Even though you're not the one that died, you become the center of attention. Everyone is looking at you. They're waiting for you to break down. You don't want to cry in front of a roomful of people, but if you don't cry, you'll look emotionless. No matter what, people are going to have something to say about you.

On that note, they don't tell you that at least one family member is bound to act like a huge asshole. You'd think that everyone would kiss and make up for the sake of the person that died, but no. Some people will have the nerve to fight over money. Fight over the will. Fight over who loved who more. Even though someone you collectively loved was ripped away from this world, the people around you will continue to fight over pointless shit.

They don't tell you how business-like death is, either. Buying a casket. Buying flowers. Buying a gravestone. You feel like you're owed all of those things, that you should get them handed to you free of charge, but you have to pay for all of it. Death is a business. Dozens of people are making money off of your misery.

They don't tell you that most of the I'm-sorry-for-your-losses and if-there's-anything-I-can-do's are empty promises. Yes, your friends are sad that you're sad. Yes, they're around if you need anyone to vent to. They'll prove that by sending you a fruit basket and showing up for the funeral, but that's about it. They don't want to help you move furniture or sell the house. They don't want to be bothered.

They don't tell you, that even though the funeral and wake lasted three excruciating days, it doesn't feel long enough after it's over. The day after it's all done, you feel like the rest of the world has moved on, even though you know you're never going to. And when you try to go about your day like usual, you feel guilty again. You feel like you should still be honoring their death.

They don't tell you that laughing is healthy for you, either. Whenever you see a funeral in the movies, the crowd is filled with straight-faced mourners. But there's nothing wrong with laughing over old memories. It might feel disrespectful, but it's not. Do you really think your loved one wants you to cry? They'd rather look down and see you smile.

23

I Root For Your Team

You loved your team. Watched every game from the living room. Cheering, booing, complaining, and cursing. When they won, it was like you had a victory of your own and when they lost, you'd still defend them, even though you admitted that they were one of the suckiest teams you've ever seen. No matter how often they lost, you wouldn't give up on them. They were the only one you would support.

You had the hats. You had the flags. You had the key chains. You had the bobbleheads. Every holiday, you'd be swamped with more merch, because everyone that knew you knew how much you loved your team.

I'm not into sports. All I know about them are what you've told me. When a baseball game comes on, I turn the channel, and when a football game comes on, I turn it even faster. At least, I used to.

Now, if I see that your team is playing, I'll pause the television for long enough to check the score. And if your team is winning (and that's what I call it. Not the New York Mets or the Miami Dolphins. Your team.) then I'll crack a smile. I don't know a thing about sports, but I know all about you, and I know how much you cared about those games.

Sometimes, I'll even leave the channel on. Listen to the claps in the crowd and the fast-talking announcer that I don't give a damn about. Because when I hear the sounds of the stadium, I can imagine that you're in the room with me. That you're cheering along with them. That I'm trying my best to ignore you while I listen to my music or read a book.

The same sounds that used to annoy the hell out of me now soothe me, because I'm not really hearing the sounds. I'm hearing your voice, screaming insults at the ref. I'm hearing you complain about all the damn commercials. I'm hearing what I never realized I'd miss hearing.

It makes me feel closer to you. If there is such a thing as heaven, if you can look down on any part of the world at any given time, then I know you're not watching me mindlessly type on a computer. You're watching that stadium. You're still cheering for your team.

So when people ask me who I root for, I don't admit that I've never actually followed sports. I just name your team. Because if you loved them, so do I.

24

It's Okay To Feel Fucked Up

I don't care if the rest of your family is handling the tragedy elegantly, without picking up a beer or cursing each other out. I don't care if they look calm and composed, even though they're secretly dying inside. Everyone handles their grief differently. If you need to act out, it doesn't mean you're a fuck-up.

Do you need to get wasted? Do you need to sleep with a stranger? Do you need to run away? Do you need to shut yourself in your room, avoiding all of your texts and phone calls? Well, whatever you feel like you have to do, do it. Get it out of your system.

It's okay to break. It's only human to lash out after you've suffered from a major loss. So don't feel guilty about waking up next to a random or going through your day with an insufferable hangover. It happens. It doesn't make you a bad person. It just makes you a person.

Even though everyone will warn you about lust and liquor, because it'll only numb your pain, sometimes you have to numb your pain. Just for a little while. And once that numbness goes away, you'll finally be ready to feel everything that you've been afraid to feel.

I'm not saying you should hit the clubs whenever you have the urge to cry. You can't put a time limit on your grief, but you have to put a time limit on your destructive behavior. Two days after the funeral, it's okay to finish off a bottle of wine by yourself. But two months after? You're veering into dangerous territory.

It's not that your grieving time is officially over after the funeral is over. You can still grieve. But try to limit that destructive behavior to once or twice a year, on their birthday and on the date of their death. Why? Because you don't want to let the sadness overpower your soul. The person you've lost wouldn't want that. They want you to be healthy.

So once you're done with your weekend of binge drinking, decide to take the healthy route. You can travel. You can paint. You can join a gym. Find a way to distract yourself while improving yourself. No, running on a treadmill isn't as easy as buying a six-pack, but it will make you feel better by the end of the day.

And you deserve to feel better.

25

You Don't Actually Want To Die

I know you're miserable. I know you're sick of feeling this way. And I know you're ready to see them again.

After everything you've been through, you probably feel like you're ready to leave this earth. After all, you don't have anything left to live for now that they're gone. You don't have a reason to get up in the morning. You don't have any reason to smile throughout the day. And sometimes, you feel like you don't have anyone left that loves you.

But no matter how intense the pain is right now, you don't want to die. You still have so much left to live for. It's a cliché, but it's a cliché, because it's true. You know the pain that yesterday brought, but you don't know about the beauty that tomorrow will bring.

If you don't want to live for yourself, then at least live for the people surrounding you. If you were gone, imagine how much pain they'd feel. You can claim that they'd be fine, that they'd get over it and would be better off without you, but you know that's a lie, because you're not over the deaths you've endured.

Live, because you have pets that would be devastated if you stopped walking through the door. Live, because you have friends that you can make laugh on their worst days. Live, because you have family members that want to hear about your love life on holidays and send you cards for your birthday.

But above all, you should live for yourself. One day, you'll take that dream vacation you've always wanted to go on. One day, you'll be able to afford that house that you've been saving up for. One day, you'll meet your forever person and will live happily ever after with them. One day, you'll be thankful that you chose to live.

Life sucks, but it doesn't suck consistently. Eventually, it will get better. Yes, there will probably be more funerals and there will definitely be more pain. But before things go downhill again, make the most of your uphill journey.

Buy tickets for that music festival you're always hearing about. Spend time with friends you haven't seen since high school. Adopt a puppy. Create a bucket list and cross off as many items as you can. Instead of wasting away inside of your house, get out and see the world—even if that means eating at the diner down the block for the very first time.

Whatever you do, don't hurt yourself. And don't wish for death. Make the loved ones you've lost proud by doing all of the things that they would be doing if they were still alive.

26

It's Time To Heal

Maybe it's been a month since their death. Maybe it's been ten years. It doesn't matter how much time has passed. If you're still struggling, that's okay. That's human.

What are you supposed to do? Once you're past the period of grieving, of crying into your pillow and screaming into the darkness, you need to get creative. The world took something important away from you and now it's time for you to bring something new into the world.

Write. Paint. Sing. Create.

Create something, even if you're a sad excuse for an artist. You don't have to show your finished work to anyone. You don't have to get your writing published or hang your artwork on the fridge. Just get all of your pent-up emotions out of your system. No amount of moping is going to help. So stop complaining about how life isn't fair and venting about how pissed off you are at the universe.

Try writing. Write a letter to someone that's passed away, even though they'll never get to read it. Tell them how much you love them, how much they mean to you, and how much you miss them. Tell them about all of the exciting things that have happened to you in the past. Treat them like they're your long lost penpal.

Or you could try writing a song. A poem. A story. A memoir. Open up a blank document on your computer and type until you feel like you've gotten everything out of your system. It doesn't need to be a masterpiece. It doesn't even need to be coherent. The point isn't to let other people know how you feel. The point is to understand how *you're* feeling and to help yourself experience something other than self-pity and despair.

If it's too hard for you to find the right words to say, then you could paint. Paint pictures of the way that their house used to look, back when they were still living in it. Paint a portrait of them from memory. Paint whatever you feel like you need to paint. Just grab a brush (or a pen or a pencil or a crayon) and let your heart guide your hand.

Stop by a craft store if you have to. Create a scrapbook filled with your favorite pictures of them. Pick up some yarn so you can crochet a blanket, the way that they used to in their free time. Buy a pottery wheel. Make a damn friendship bracelet if you have to. Just create *something* that'll give you an outlet for your grief. Create something that'll keep your hands busy and your mind busy.

You can't control what the world takes away from you, but you *can* control what you bring into the world.

About the Author

Holly Riordan is a Thought Catalog employee who writes articles about love and sex by day and short stories about blood and guts by night.

Thought Catalog, it's a website.
www.thoughtcatalog.com

Social
facebook.com/thoughtcatalog
twitter.com/thoughtcatalog
tumblr.com/thoughtcatalog
instagram.com/thoughtcatalog

Corporate
www.thought.is

89514534R00052

Made in the USA
Middletown, DE
17 September 2018